This Meal Planner

Belongs To:

_____

Weekly Meal Planning

	Breakfast	Lunch	Dinner	Snacks
Monday				
Tuesday				
Wednesday				
Thursday				
Friday				

Week Of: _____

	Breakfast	Lunch	Dinner	Snacks
Saturday				
Sunday				

Weekly Shopping List

☐	☐	☐
☐	☐	☐
☐	☐	☐
☐	☐	☐
☐	☐	☐
☐	☐	☐
☐	☐	☐
☐	☐	☐
☐	☐	☐
☐	☐	☐

Weekly Meal Planning

	Breakfast	Lunch	Dinner	Snacks
Monday				
Tuesday				
Wednesday				
Thursday				
Friday				

Week Of: _____

	Breakfast	Lunch	Dinner	Snacks
Saturday				
Sunday				

Weekly Shopping List

☐	☐	☐
☐	☐	☐
☐	☐	☐
☐	☐	☐
☐	☐	☐
☐	☐	☐
☐	☐	☐
☐	☐	☐
☐	☐	☐
☐	☐	☐

Weekly Meal Planning

	Breakfast	Lunch	Dinner	Snacks
Monday				
Tuesday				
Wednesday				
Thursday				
Friday				

Week Of: _____

	Breakfast	Lunch	Dinner	Snacks
Saturday				
Sunday				

Weekly Shopping List

☐	☐	☐
☐	☐	☐
☐	☐	☐
☐	☐	☐
☐	☐	☐
☐	☐	☐
☐	☐	☐
☐	☐	☐
☐	☐	☐
☐	☐	☐

Weekly Meal Planning

	Breakfast	Lunch	Dinner	Snacks
Monday				
Tuesday				
Wednesday				
Thursday				
Friday				

Week Of: _____

	Breakfast	Lunch	Dinner	Snacks
Saturday				
Sunday				

Weekly Shopping List

☐	☐	☐
☐	☐	☐
☐	☐	☐
☐	☐	☐
☐	☐	☐
☐	☐	☐
☐	☐	☐
☐	☐	☐
☐	☐	☐
☐	☐	☐

Weekly Meal Planning

	Breakfast	Lunch	Dinner	Snacks
Monday				
Tuesday				
Wednesday				
Thursday				
Friday				

Week Of: _____

	Breakfast	Lunch	Dinner	Snacks
Saturday				
Sunday				

Weekly Shopping List

☐	☐	☐
☐	☐	☐
☐	☐	☐
☐	☐	☐
☐	☐	☐
☐	☐	☐
☐	☐	☐
☐	☐	☐
☐	☐	☐
☐	☐	☐

Weekly Meal Planning

	Breakfast	Lunch	Dinner	Snacks
Monday				
Tuesday				
Wednesday				
Thursday				
Friday				

Week Of: _____

	Breakfast	Lunch	Dinner	Snacks
Saturday				
Sunday				

Weekly Shopping List

☐	☐	☐
☐	☐	☐
☐	☐	☐
☐	☐	☐
☐	☐	☐
☐	☐	☐
☐	☐	☐
☐	☐	☐
☐	☐	☐
☐	☐	☐

Weekly Meal Planning

	Breakfast	Lunch	Dinner	Snacks
Monday				
Tuesday				
Wednesday				
Thursday				
Friday				

Week Of: _____

	Breakfast	Lunch	Dinner	Snacks
Saturday				
Sunday				

Weekly Shopping List

☐	☐	☐
☐	☐	☐
☐	☐	☐
☐	☐	☐
☐	☐	☐
☐	☐	☐
☐	☐	☐
☐	☐	☐
☐	☐	☐
☐	☐	☐

Weekly Meal Planning

	Breakfast	Lunch	Dinner	Snacks
Monday				
Tuesday				
Wednesday				
Thursday				
Friday				

Week Of: _____

	Breakfast	Lunch	Dinner	Snacks
Saturday				
Sunday				

Weekly Shopping List

☐	☐	☐
☐	☐	☐
☐	☐	☐
☐	☐	☐
☐	☐	☐
☐	☐	☐
☐	☐	☐
☐	☐	☐
☐	☐	☐
☐	☐	☐

Weekly Meal Planning

	Breakfast	Lunch	Dinner	Snacks
Monday				
Tuesday				
Wednesday				
Thursday				
Friday				

Week Of: _____

	Breakfast	Lunch	Dinner	Snacks
Saturday				
Sunday				

Weekly Shopping List

☐	☐	☐
☐	☐	☐
☐	☐	☐
☐	☐	☐
☐	☐	☐
☐	☐	☐
☐	☐	☐
☐	☐	☐
☐	☐	☐
☐	☐	☐

Weekly Meal Planning

	Breakfast	Lunch	Dinner	Snacks
Monday				
Tuesday				
Wednesday				
Thursday				
Friday				

Week Of: _____

	Breakfast	Lunch	Dinner	Snacks
Saturday				
Sunday				

Weekly Shopping List

☐	☐	☐
☐	☐	☐
☐	☐	☐
☐	☐	☐
☐	☐	☐
☐	☐	☐
☐	☐	☐
☐	☐	☐
☐	☐	☐
☐	☐	☐

Weekly Meal Planning

	Breakfast	Lunch	Dinner	Snacks
Monday				
Tuesday				
Wednesday				
Thursday				
Friday				

Week Of: _____

	Breakfast	Lunch	Dinner	Snacks
Saturday				
Sunday				

Weekly Shopping List

☐	☐	☐
☐	☐	☐
☐	☐	☐
☐	☐	☐
☐	☐	☐
☐	☐	☐
☐	☐	☐
☐	☐	☐
☐	☐	☐
☐	☐	☐

Weekly Meal Planning

	Breakfast	Lunch	Dinner	Snacks
Monday				
Tuesday				
Wednesday				
Thursday				
Friday				

Week Of: _____

	Breakfast	Lunch	Dinner	Snacks
Saturday				
Sunday				

Weekly Shopping List

☐	☐	☐
☐	☐	☐
☐	☐	☐
☐	☐	☐
☐	☐	☐
☐	☐	☐
☐	☐	☐
☐	☐	☐
☐	☐	☐
☐	☐	☐

Weekly Meal Planning

	Breakfast	Lunch	Dinner	Snacks
Monday				
Tuesday				
Wednesday				
Thursday				
Friday				

Week Of: _____

	Breakfast	Lunch	Dinner	Snacks
Saturday				
Sunday				

Weekly Shopping List

☐	☐	☐
☐	☐	☐
☐	☐	☐
☐	☐	☐
☐	☐	☐
☐	☐	☐
☐	☐	☐
☐	☐	☐
☐	☐	☐
☐	☐	☐

Weekly Meal Planning

	Breakfast	Lunch	Dinner	Snacks
Monday				
Tuesday				
Wednesday				
Thursday				
Friday				

Week Of: _____

	Breakfast	Lunch	Dinner	Snacks
Saturday				
Sunday				

Weekly Shopping List

☐	☐	☐
☐	☐	☐
☐	☐	☐
☐	☐	☐
☐	☐	☐
☐	☐	☐
☐	☐	☐
☐	☐	☐
☐	☐	☐
☐	☐	☐

Weekly Meal Planning

	Breakfast	Lunch	Dinner	Snacks
Monday				
Tuesday				
Wednesday				
Thursday				
Friday				

Week Of: _____

	Breakfast	Lunch	Dinner	Snacks
Saturday				
Sunday				

Weekly Shopping List

☐	☐	☐
☐	☐	☐
☐	☐	☐
☐	☐	☐
☐	☐	☐
☐	☐	☐
☐	☐	☐
☐	☐	☐
☐	☐	☐
☐	☐	☐

Weekly Meal Planning

	Breakfast	Lunch	Dinner	Snacks
Monday				
Tuesday				
Wednesday				
Thursday				
Friday				

Week Of: _____

	Breakfast	Lunch	Dinner	Snacks
Saturday				
Sunday				

Weekly Shopping List

☐	☐	☐
☐	☐	☐
☐	☐	☐
☐	☐	☐
☐	☐	☐
☐	☐	☐
☐	☐	☐
☐	☐	☐
☐	☐	☐
☐	☐	☐

Weekly Meal Planning

	Breakfast	Lunch	Dinner	Snacks
Monday				
Tuesday				
Wednesday				
Thursday				
Friday				

Week Of: _____

	Breakfast	Lunch	Dinner	Snacks
Saturday				
Sunday				

Weekly Shopping List

☐	☐	☐
☐	☐	☐
☐	☐	☐
☐	☐	☐
☐	☐	☐
☐	☐	☐
☐	☐	☐
☐	☐	☐
☐	☐	☐
☐	☐	☐

Weekly Meal Planning

	Breakfast	Lunch	Dinner	Snacks
Monday				
Tuesday				
Wednesday				
Thursday				
Friday				

Week Of: _____

	Breakfast	Lunch	Dinner	Snacks
Saturday				
Sunday				

Weekly Shopping List

☐	☐	☐
☐	☐	☐
☐	☐	☐
☐	☐	☐
☐	☐	☐
☐	☐	☐
☐	☐	☐
☐	☐	☐
☐	☐	☐
☐	☐	☐

Weekly Meal Planning

	Breakfast	Lunch	Dinner	Snacks
Monday				
Tuesday				
Wednesday				
Thursday				
Friday				

Week Of: _____

	Breakfast	Lunch	Dinner	Snacks
Saturday				
Sunday				

Weekly Shopping List

☐	☐	☐
☐	☐	☐
☐	☐	☐
☐	☐	☐
☐	☐	☐
☐	☐	☐
☐	☐	☐
☐	☐	☐
☐	☐	☐
☐	☐	☐

Weekly Meal Planning

	Breakfast	Lunch	Dinner	Snacks
Monday				
Tuesday				
Wednesday				
Thursday				
Friday				

Week Of: _____

	Breakfast	Lunch	Dinner	Snacks
Saturday				
Sunday				

Weekly Shopping List

☐	☐	☐
☐	☐	☐
☐	☐	☐
☐	☐	☐
☐	☐	☐
☐	☐	☐
☐	☐	☐
☐	☐	☐
☐	☐	☐
☐	☐	☐

Weekly Meal Planning

	Breakfast	Lunch	Dinner	Snacks
Monday				
Tuesday				
Wednesday				
Thursday				
Friday				

Week Of: _____

	Breakfast	Lunch	Dinner	Snacks
Saturday				
Sunday				

Weekly Shopping List

☐	☐	☐
☐	☐	☐
☐	☐	☐
☐	☐	☐
☐	☐	☐
☐	☐	☐
☐	☐	☐
☐	☐	☐
☐	☐	☐
☐	☐	☐

Weekly Meal Planning

	Breakfast	Lunch	Dinner	Snacks
Monday				
Tuesday				
Wednesday				
Thursday				
Friday				

Week Of: _____

	Breakfast	Lunch	Dinner	Snacks
Saturday				
Sunday				

Weekly Shopping List

☐	☐	☐
☐	☐	☐
☐	☐	☐
☐	☐	☐
☐	☐	☐
☐	☐	☐
☐	☐	☐
☐	☐	☐
☐	☐	☐
☐	☐	☐

Weekly Meal Planning

	Breakfast	Lunch	Dinner	Snacks
Monday				
Tuesday				
Wednesday				
Thursday				
Friday				

Week Of: _____

	Breakfast	Lunch	Dinner	Snacks
Saturday				
Sunday				

Weekly Shopping List

☐	☐	☐
☐	☐	☐
☐	☐	☐
☐	☐	☐
☐	☐	☐
☐	☐	☐
☐	☐	☐
☐	☐	☐
☐	☐	☐
☐	☐	☐

Weekly Meal Planning

	Breakfast	Lunch	Dinner	Snacks
Monday				
Tuesday				
Wednesday				
Thursday				
Friday				

Week Of: _____

	Breakfast	Lunch	Dinner	Snacks
Saturday				
Sunday				

Weekly Shopping List

☐	☐	☐
☐	☐	☐
☐	☐	☐
☐	☐	☐
☐	☐	☐
☐	☐	☐
☐	☐	☐
☐	☐	☐
☐	☐	☐
☐	☐	☐

Weekly Meal Planning

	Breakfast	Lunch	Dinner	Snacks
Monday				
Tuesday				
Wednesday				
Thursday				
Friday				

Week Of: _____

	Breakfast	Lunch	Dinner	Snacks
Saturday				
Sunday				

Weekly Shopping List

☐	☐	☐
☐	☐	☐
☐	☐	☐
☐	☐	☐
☐	☐	☐
☐	☐	☐
☐	☐	☐
☐	☐	☐
☐	☐	☐
☐	☐	☐

Weekly Meal Planning

	Breakfast	Lunch	Dinner	Snacks
Monday				
Tuesday				
Wednesday				
Thursday				
Friday				

Week Of: _____

	Breakfast	Lunch	Dinner	Snacks
Saturday				
Sunday				

Weekly Shopping List

☐	☐	☐
☐	☐	☐
☐	☐	☐
☐	☐	☐
☐	☐	☐
☐	☐	☐
☐	☐	☐
☐	☐	☐
☐	☐	☐
☐	☐	☐

Weekly Meal Planning

	Breakfast	Lunch	Dinner	Snacks
Monday				
Tuesday				
Wednesday				
Thursday				
Friday				

Week Of: _____

	Breakfast	Lunch	Dinner	Snacks
Saturday				
Sunday				

Weekly Shopping List

☐	☐	☐
☐	☐	☐
☐	☐	☐
☐	☐	☐
☐	☐	☐
☐	☐	☐
☐	☐	☐
☐	☐	☐
☐	☐	☐
☐	☐	☐

Weekly Meal Planning

	Breakfast	Lunch	Dinner	Snacks
Monday				
Tuesday				
Wednesday				
Thursday				
Friday				

Week Of: _____

	Breakfast	Lunch	Dinner	Snacks
Saturday				
Sunday				

Weekly Shopping List

☐	☐	☐
☐	☐	☐
☐	☐	☐
☐	☐	☐
☐	☐	☐
☐	☐	☐
☐	☐	☐
☐	☐	☐
☐	☐	☐
☐	☐	☐

Weekly Meal Planning

	Breakfast	Lunch	Dinner	Snacks
Monday				
Tuesday				
Wednesday				
Thursday				
Friday				

Week Of: _____

	Breakfast	Lunch	Dinner	Snacks
Saturday				
Sunday				

Weekly Shopping List

☐	☐	☐
☐	☐	☐
☐	☐	☐
☐	☐	☐
☐	☐	☐
☐	☐	☐
☐	☐	☐
☐	☐	☐
☐	☐	☐
☐	☐	☐

Weekly Meal Planning

	Breakfast	Lunch	Dinner	Snacks
Monday				
Tuesday				
Wednesday				
Thursday				
Friday				

Week Of: _____

	Breakfast	Lunch	Dinner	Snacks
Saturday				
Sunday				

Weekly Shopping List

☐	☐	☐
☐	☐	☐
☐	☐	☐
☐	☐	☐
☐	☐	☐
☐	☐	☐
☐	☐	☐
☐	☐	☐
☐	☐	☐
☐	☐	☐

Weekly Meal Planning

	Breakfast	Lunch	Dinner	Snacks
Monday				
Tuesday				
Wednesday				
Thursday				
Friday				

Week Of: _____

	Breakfast	Lunch	Dinner	Snacks
Saturday				
Sunday				

Weekly Shopping List

☐	☐	☐
☐	☐	☐
☐	☐	☐
☐	☐	☐
☐	☐	☐
☐	☐	☐
☐	☐	☐
☐	☐	☐
☐	☐	☐
☐	☐	☐

Weekly Meal Planning

	Breakfast	Lunch	Dinner	Snacks
Monday				
Tuesday				
Wednesday				
Thursday				
Friday				

Week Of: _____

	Breakfast	Lunch	Dinner	Snacks
Saturday				
Sunday				

Weekly Shopping List

☐	☐	☐
☐	☐	☐
☐	☐	☐
☐	☐	☐
☐	☐	☐
☐	☐	☐
☐	☐	☐
☐	☐	☐
☐	☐	☐
☐	☐	☐

Weekly Meal Planning

	Breakfast	Lunch	Dinner	Snacks
Monday				
Tuesday				
Wednesday				
Thursday				
Friday				

Week Of: _____

	Breakfast	Lunch	Dinner	Snacks
Saturday				
Sunday				

Weekly Shopping List

☐	☐	☐
☐	☐	☐
☐	☐	☐
☐	☐	☐
☐	☐	☐
☐	☐	☐
☐	☐	☐
☐	☐	☐
☐	☐	☐
☐	☐	☐

Weekly Meal Planning

	Breakfast	Lunch	Dinner	Snacks
Monday				
Tuesday				
Wednesday				
Thursday				
Friday				

Week Of: _____

	Breakfast	Lunch	Dinner	Snacks
Saturday				
Sunday				

Weekly Shopping List

☐	☐	☐
☐	☐	☐
☐	☐	☐
☐	☐	☐
☐	☐	☐
☐	☐	☐
☐	☐	☐
☐	☐	☐
☐	☐	☐
☐	☐	☐

Weekly Meal Planning

	Breakfast	Lunch	Dinner	Snacks
Monday				
Tuesday				
Wednesday				
Thursday				
Friday				

Week Of: _____

	Breakfast	Lunch	Dinner	Snacks
Saturday				
Sunday				

Weekly Shopping List

☐	☐	☐
☐	☐	☐
☐	☐	☐
☐	☐	☐
☐	☐	☐
☐	☐	☐
☐	☐	☐
☐	☐	☐
☐	☐	☐
☐	☐	☐

Weekly Meal Planning

	Breakfast	Lunch	Dinner	Snacks
Monday				
Tuesday				
Wednesday				
Thursday				
Friday				

Week Of: _____

	Breakfast	Lunch	Dinner	Snacks
Saturday				
Sunday				

Weekly Shopping List

☐	☐	☐
☐	☐	☐
☐	☐	☐
☐	☐	☐
☐	☐	☐
☐	☐	☐
☐	☐	☐
☐	☐	☐
☐	☐	☐
☐	☐	☐

Weekly Meal Planning

	Breakfast	Lunch	Dinner	Snacks
Monday				
Tuesday				
Wednesday				
Thursday				
Friday				

Week Of: _____

	Breakfast	Lunch	Dinner	Snacks
Saturday				
Sunday				

Weekly Shopping List

☐	☐	☐
☐	☐	☐
☐	☐	☐
☐	☐	☐
☐	☐	☐
☐	☐	☐
☐	☐	☐
☐	☐	☐
☐	☐	☐
☐	☐	☐

Weekly Meal Planning

	Breakfast	Lunch	Dinner	Snacks
Monday				
Tuesday				
Wednesday				
Thursday				
Friday				

Week Of: _____

	Breakfast	Lunch	Dinner	Snacks
Saturday				
Sunday				

Weekly Shopping List

☐	☐	☐
☐	☐	☐
☐	☐	☐
☐	☐	☐
☐	☐	☐
☐	☐	☐
☐	☐	☐
☐	☐	☐
☐	☐	☐
☐	☐	☐

Weekly Meal Planning

	Breakfast	Lunch	Dinner	Snacks
Monday				
Tuesday				
Wednesday				
Thursday				
Friday				

Week Of: _____

	Breakfast	Lunch	Dinner	Snacks
Saturday				
Sunday				

Weekly Shopping List

☐	☐	☐
☐	☐	☐
☐	☐	☐
☐	☐	☐
☐	☐	☐
☐	☐	☐
☐	☐	☐
☐	☐	☐
☐	☐	☐
☐	☐	☐

Weekly Meal Planning

	Breakfast	Lunch	Dinner	Snacks
Monday				
Tuesday				
Wednesday				
Thursday				
Friday				

Week Of: _____

	Breakfast	Lunch	Dinner	Snacks
Saturday				
Sunday				

Weekly Shopping List

☐	☐	☐
☐	☐	☐
☐	☐	☐
☐	☐	☐
☐	☐	☐
☐	☐	☐
☐	☐	☐
☐	☐	☐
☐	☐	☐
☐	☐	☐

Weekly Meal Planning

	Breakfast	Lunch	Dinner	Snacks
Monday				
Tuesday				
Wednesday				
Thursday				
Friday				

Week Of: _____

	Breakfast	Lunch	Dinner	Snacks
Saturday				
Sunday				

Weekly Shopping List

☐	☐	☐
☐	☐	☐
☐	☐	☐
☐	☐	☐
☐	☐	☐
☐	☐	☐
☐	☐	☐
☐	☐	☐
☐	☐	☐
☐	☐	☐

Weekly Meal Planning

	Breakfast	Lunch	Dinner	Snacks
Monday				
Tuesday				
Wednesday				
Thursday				
Friday				

Week Of: _____

	Breakfast	Lunch	Dinner	Snacks
Saturday				
Sunday				

Weekly Shopping List

☐	☐	☐
☐	☐	☐
☐	☐	☐
☐	☐	☐
☐	☐	☐
☐	☐	☐
☐	☐	☐
☐	☐	☐
☐	☐	☐
☐	☐	☐

Weekly Meal Planning

	Breakfast	Lunch	Dinner	Snacks
Monday				
Tuesday				
Wednesday				
Thursday				
Friday				

Week Of: _____

	Breakfast	Lunch	Dinner	Snacks
Saturday				
Sunday				

Weekly Shopping List

☐	☐	☐
☐	☐	☐
☐	☐	☐
☐	☐	☐
☐	☐	☐
☐	☐	☐
☐	☐	☐
☐	☐	☐
☐	☐	☐
☐	☐	☐

Weekly Meal Planning

	Breakfast	Lunch	Dinner	Snacks
Monday				
Tuesday				
Wednesday				
Thursday				
Friday				

Week Of: _____

	Breakfast	Lunch	Dinner	Snacks
Saturday				
Sunday				

Weekly Shopping List

☐	☐	☐
☐	☐	☐
☐	☐	☐
☐	☐	☐
☐	☐	☐
☐	☐	☐
☐	☐	☐
☐	☐	☐
☐	☐	☐
☐	☐	☐

Weekly Meal Planning

	Breakfast	Lunch	Dinner	Snacks
Monday				
Tuesday				
Wednesday				
Thursday				
Friday				

Week Of: _____

	Breakfast	Lunch	Dinner	Snacks
Saturday				
Sunday				

Weekly Shopping List

☐	☐	☐
☐	☐	☐
☐	☐	☐
☐	☐	☐
☐	☐	☐
☐	☐	☐
☐	☐	☐
☐	☐	☐
☐	☐	☐
☐	☐	☐

Weekly Meal Planning

	Breakfast	Lunch	Dinner	Snacks
Monday				
Tuesday				
Wednesday				
Thursday				
Friday				

Week Of: _____

	Breakfast	Lunch	Dinner	Snacks
Saturday				
Sunday				

Weekly Shopping List

☐	☐	☐
☐	☐	☐
☐	☐	☐
☐	☐	☐
☐	☐	☐
☐	☐	☐
☐	☐	☐
☐	☐	☐
☐	☐	☐
☐	☐	☐

Weekly Meal Planning

	Breakfast	Lunch	Dinner	Snacks
Monday				
Tuesday				
Wednesday				
Thursday				
Friday				

Week Of: _____

	Breakfast	Lunch	Dinner	Snacks
Saturday				
Sunday				

Weekly Shopping List

☐	☐	☐
☐	☐	☐
☐	☐	☐
☐	☐	☐
☐	☐	☐
☐	☐	☐
☐	☐	☐
☐	☐	☐
☐	☐	☐
☐	☐	☐

Weekly Meal Planning

	Breakfast	Lunch	Dinner	Snacks
Monday				
Tuesday				
Wednesday				
Thursday				
Friday				

Week Of: _____

	Breakfast	Lunch	Dinner	Snacks
Saturday				
Sunday				

Weekly Shopping List

☐	☐	☐
☐	☐	☐
☐	☐	☐
☐	☐	☐
☐	☐	☐
☐	☐	☐
☐	☐	☐
☐	☐	☐
☐	☐	☐
☐	☐	☐

Weekly Meal Planning

	Breakfast	Lunch	Dinner	Snacks
Monday				
Tuesday				
Wednesday				
Thursday				
Friday				

Week Of: _____

	Breakfast	Lunch	Dinner	Snacks
Saturday				
Sunday				

Weekly Shopping List

☐	☐	☐
☐	☐	☐
☐	☐	☐
☐	☐	☐
☐	☐	☐
☐	☐	☐
☐	☐	☐
☐	☐	☐
☐	☐	☐
☐	☐	☐

Weekly Meal Planning

	Breakfast	Lunch	Dinner	Snacks
Monday				
Tuesday				
Wednesday				
Thursday				
Friday				

Week Of: _____

	Breakfast	Lunch	Dinner	Snacks
Saturday				
Sunday				

Weekly Shopping List

☐	☐	☐
☐	☐	☐
☐	☐	☐
☐	☐	☐
☐	☐	☐
☐	☐	☐
☐	☐	☐
☐	☐	☐
☐	☐	☐
☐	☐	☐

Weekly Meal Planning

	Breakfast	Lunch	Dinner	Snacks
Monday				
Tuesday				
Wednesday				
Thursday				
Friday				

Week Of: _____

	Breakfast	Lunch	Dinner	Snacks
Saturday				
Sunday				

Weekly Shopping List

☐	☐	☐
☐	☐	☐
☐	☐	☐
☐	☐	☐
☐	☐	☐
☐	☐	☐
☐	☐	☐
☐	☐	☐
☐	☐	☐
☐	☐	☐

Weekly Meal Planning

	Breakfast	Lunch	Dinner	Snacks
Monday				
Tuesday				
Wednesday				
Thursday				
Friday				

Week Of: _____

	Breakfast	Lunch	Dinner	Snacks
Saturday				
Sunday				

Weekly Shopping List

☐	☐	☐
☐	☐	☐
☐	☐	☐
☐	☐	☐
☐	☐	☐
☐	☐	☐
☐	☐	☐
☐	☐	☐
☐	☐	☐
☐	☐	☐

Recipe Name: _____

Ingredients:

Instructions:

Recipe Name: _____

Ingredients:

Instructions:

Recipe Name: _____

Ingredients:

Instructions:

Recipe Name: _____

Ingredients:

Instructions:

Recipe Name: _____

Ingredients:

Instructions:

Recipe Name: _____

Ingredients:

Instructions:

Recipe Name: _____

Ingredients:

Instructions:

Recipe Name: _____

Ingredients:

Instructions:

Recipe Name: _____

Ingredients:

Instructions:

Recipe Name: _____

Ingredients:

Instructions:

Recipe Name: _____

Ingredients:

Instructions:

Recipe Name: _____

Ingredients:

Instructions:

Recipe Name: _____

Ingredients:

Instructions:

Recipe Name: _____

Ingredients:

Instructions:

Recipe Name: _____

Ingredients:

Instructions:

Recipe Name: _____

Ingredients:

Instructions:

Recipe Name: _____

Ingredients:

Instructions:

Recipe Name: _____

Ingredients:

Instructions:

Recipe Name: _____

Ingredients:

Instructions:

Recipe Name: _____

Ingredients:

Instructions:

Made in the USA
Columbia, SC
17 February 2025